AF316602

Monarch Butterfly 123

Written and Illustrated
by PJ Kennedy

About the Author

Parent. Artist. Advocate. Social Worker.

As a parent, I often look for and appreciate the simple things in life. I strive to teach my children about the interaction people have with the planet and all living things. I want them to learn how making small changes, like in your garden, can have a big impact and how they can be a part of making the world a better place for them and future generations.

Several years ago I tried growing milkweed in my garden and fell in love with the cause of helping the Monarch Butterfly population. Planting Milkweed is important because Monarch Butterflies only lay their eggs on these plants. Once the egg hatches and a tiny caterpillar emerges, it survives by eating any part of the milkweed plant. I thought, if I could grow milkweed in my garden, surely I would encourage butterflies to visit, so I planted some seeds and waited. As the seeds grew into plants I checked them every day, hoping for a monarch egg to show up. One day I was searching in my garden and I saw a small monarch egg on the underside of one of the milkweed leaves. It was soon after, I discovered a fat monarch caterpillar had been living in my garden and was ready to pupate into a chrysalis. From that point on, I was hooked.

Fast forward a few years, and I now spend many hours a week, during the summer, hunting for monarch eggs. I scan the leaves of milkweed plants that I find on the side of the road, in parks, and in people's yards. I tell anyone who will listen about the importance of milkweed.

This passion for the Monarch Butterfly has led me to learn about other practices that encourage the survival of all pollinator populations. And thus, the idea for a 123 book about Monarch Butterflies came to be!

one
One
One monarch butterfly
1

two

two

Two milkweed plants emerging from the ground

three

three

3

Three coneflowers ready to feed the butterflies

Four monarch butterfly eggs were laid on milkweed leaves

Five monarch caterpillars at different stages of growth. These stages are called "instars".

6

six

six

Six full-grown monarch caterpillars

seven

Seven caterpillars preparing to pupate into chrysalis'.

eight

eight

Eight chrysalises hanging on a branch

nine

nine

9

Nine chrysalises with butterflies preparing to hatch

Ten butterflies that just hatched

eleven

eleven

11

Eleven milkweed leaves ready for more butterflies and caterpillars

Twelve seed pods are starting to grow.

thirteen

thirteen

13

Thirteen new eggs are laid on the milkweed. After a few days, tiny caterpillars will emerge.

fourteen

fourteen

14

Fourteen seed pods are on the plants

Fifteen monarchs begin their journey south as the growing season ends.

sixteen

sixteen

16

Sixteen milkweed seeds blow away once the seed pod dries and cracks open.

seventeen
seventeen

17

Seventeen seeds are collected and saved for the next growing season.

eighteen

eighteen

18

Eighteen spring seedling cups are ready to be filled with dirt and seeds sown.

nineteen

nineteen

19

Nineteen drops of water fall onto the newly planted seeds, which will help them grow.

twenty

twenty

20

Twenty milkweed seedlings are ready to transplant.

Other Facts

Monarchs can travel on average 50 miles a day when migrating

A monarch caterpillar may travel over 30 ft to find the perfect spot to make a chrysalis

Monarchs have a difficult time flying when the temperature is lower than 55 degress f.

There are over 73 species of Milkweed Native to North America

A migrating monarch will travel over 2,000 miles before it is in its final resting spot. Many generations winter in the same trees as their ancestors

Less than 5% of monarch caterpillars reach the adult stage of a monarch butterfly

How can I help?

Plant milkweed that is native to your region

Start a pollinator garden full of plants that offer nectar and shelter to butterflies, including milkweed

Teach others about monarchs and their importance to our ecosystem

Do not use pesticides on your garden, yard or flowers. Pesticides are harmful to butterflies and caterpillars